Learning to Pray the Lord's Prayer

Jason Staggers

ASCEND PRESS

Copyright © 2025 by Jason Staggers

All rights reserved. No part of this publication may be reproduced, stored or transmitted in any form or by any means, electronic, mechanical, photocopying, recording, scanning, or otherwise without written permission from the publisher. It is illegal to copy this book, post it to a website, or distribute it by any other means without permission.

Cover artwork: *The fresco of prayer of Jesus in Gethsemane garden in the church Dreifaltigkeit-skirche* by August Müller (1923), used with permission.

This book is dedicated to my grandmothers:
Marjorie Staggers and Dorothy Clark.

If it's true as John Wesley said, that "God does nothing except in answer to believing prayer," then I am surely a follower of Christ today because of the persistent, believing prayers of these two faithful women.

Matthew 6:5–15 (ESV)

⁵ "And when you pray, you must not be like the hypocrites. For they love to stand and pray in the synagogues and at the street corners, that they may be seen by others. Truly, I say to you, they have received their reward. ⁶ But when you pray, go into your room and shut the door and pray to your Father who is in secret. And your Father who sees in secret will reward you.

⁷ "And when you pray, do not heap up empty phrases as the Gentiles do, for they think that they will be heard for their many words. ⁸ Do not be like them, for your Father knows what you need before you ask him. ⁹ Pray then like this:

"Our Father in heaven,

hallowed be your name.

¹⁰ Your kingdom come,

your will be done,

on earth as it is in heaven.

¹¹ Give us this day our daily bread,

¹² and forgive us our debts,

as we also have forgiven our debtors.

¹³ And lead us not into temptation,

but deliver us from evil.

For yours is the kingdom and the power and the glory, forever. Amen

¹⁴ For if you forgive others their trespasses, your heavenly Father will also forgive you, ¹⁵ but if you do not forgive others their trespasses, neither will your Father forgive your trespasses.

Contents

Acknowledgements	VI
Introduction	1
1. First Things First Prayers of Adoration and Worship	11
2. Prioritising God's Desires Kingdom-Centred Missional Prayers	25
3. Looking to God as Provider Prayers for Personal Provision	41
4. Reconciliation with God and People Receiving and Giving Forgiveness in Prayer	53
5. Overcoming the Darkness Prayers for Freedom and Deliverance	69
6. Finishing Strong Prayers of Praise	84
7. Developing a Discipline of Daily Prayer Putting It All Into Practice	91
About the author	97

Acknowledgements

To my beloved wife, Olivia - my greatest encourager and most loyal companion.

To my children, who I hope, more than anyone else, will live out the words of the following pages.

To my church family at ASCEND, who, in celebration of my sermon series on the Lord's Prayer, gave me the courage to put these words into print. This book is written primarily for you, and for all we will together reach for the Lord.

Introduction

An Invitation into True Relationship with God

I first began to follow Jesus nearly thirty years ago. Not long after I committed my life to Christ, my Southern Baptist grandmother gave me a short devotional book she had used to strengthen her own relationship with God. Each daily devo included a Scripture passage, reflections, application questions, and a written prayer to read from the heart.

Developing this daily habit of spending time with God has been my most important personal discipline. Whether using a tool like that devotional, a Bible reading plan, or a verse-of-the-day app, time with God in the Word and prayer is crucial for every follower of Jesus.

But I must confess, I've always found it easier to study the Bible than to pray. Prayer requires that we move from the realm of the intellect to the realm of relationship. Prayer cultivates deep connection with God.

In Acts 2:42, we read that the early church devoted themselves to four practices: the apostles' teaching, fellowship, meals together, and prayer. These were not religious checklists, but the lifelines of a Spirit-filled community. If we want to see God's power in our churches today, we must return to these ancient practices, and none is more challenging than prayer.

It's no exaggeration to say that a desire to learn to pray is one of the greatest pieces of evidence that we love God. Notice I said, "desire." Few, if any, of us have arrived. But the starting point is desire.

This book is your invitation to a journey deeper into prayer. Like every journey worthy of our time, this one begins with the words of Jesus. Before you read any further, take a moment in prayer to echo the request of Jesus' first disciples when they asked Him, *"Lord, teach us to pray."*

Becoming a "Black Belt" in Prayer

One of my hobbies is training Brazilian Jiu-Jitsu (BJJ). It's great exercise, it keeps me connected to people outside my church, and it helps relieve a lot of stress. In BJJ, earning a black belt is a mark of mastery that requires thousands of hours of training over about 10-12 years. Yet even then, black belts tend to say something like, "The more I train, the more I realise how much I have to learn."

Prayer is the same. It's a discipline we can spend our lives learning, and yet still feel like we've barely scratched the surface of what's possible.

The great English pastor and theologian Martin Lloyd-Jones, himself a great man of prayer, wrote about this very idea,

> *"I have always hesitated to deal with this subject [of prayer]. I have preached on prayer when it has come in a passage through which I have been working; but I have never presumed to produce a book on prayer, or*

even a booklet. Certain people have done this in a very mechanical manner, taking us through the different aspects, and classifying it all. It all seems so simple. But prayer is not simple."

Dr. Martin Lloyd-Jones

While prayer requires discipline, it cannot be reduced to a formula. It is the highest activity of the human soul – a deeply relational act that defies rigid structures. Yet, like any discipline, it's one we can grow in, if we will apply ourselves.

I've prayed almost daily for nearly thirty years, but recently, I've experienced growth in the quality of my own prayer life. I can see one primary reason for this - it has come as a direct result of putting focused effort into learning how to pray the Lord's Prayer.

Since I began using the Lord's Prayer as a guide for my own prayer time, I've found that I'm less easily distracted, I'm more consistent, and there's greater breadth to what I pray about. As a result, I've found greater freedom in prayer, and I even find myself sometimes getting lost in prayer.

I'm far from a black belt, but it feels as if I've tapped into a power in prayer that I didn't know was there. But it shouldn't surprise us that the Lord's Prayer could take us deeper – it is after all the Master's own teaching on prayer.

From Superstition to Structure

In high school, before our most important baseball games (not all of them), my teammates and I would huddle up and pray the Lord's Prayer. None of us were believers. It was more superstition than faith, like a good luck charm.

I've spoken to many who've had a similar relationship to the Lord's Prayer. They somehow ended up memorising it, but they were never taught how to use it as a structure or guide for how to pray.

Just like with anything, if we're going to get better at something, we need some structure.

My sons have recently started lifting weights. Showing up at the gym is a great first step, but a gym membership doesn't benefit much until you have a clear plan for how to use the equipment at the gym.

Before my sons' first gym session, we sat down together to create a workout routine that could guide them. We split their sessions into upper and lower body workouts. We identified which exercises they should do for each muscle group, and we worked out how many reps and sets to complete.

Sometimes we come to prayer like someone walking into a gym without a routine. We end up wandering around, throwing up a few proverbial prayer weights, but make little progress building prayer muscles.

The primary reason that Jesus gave His disciples the Lord's Prayer was to provide some much-needed structure – a routine for prayer that shows not only *what* to pray, but also *how* and *in what order* to pray.

The Prayer of the Ages

Throughout all of church history, the Lord's Prayer has been used as a *pattern* for prayer. Listen to what some of the spiritual giants of the past have said about praying the Lord's Prayer:

> *"To this day I am still nursing myself on the Lord's Prayer like a child and am still eating and drinking of it like an old man without getting bored of it."*

INTRODUCTION

Martin Luther

"Run through all the words of the holy prayers in Scripture, and I do not think you will find anything that is not contained in the Lord's Prayer."

Augustine

"The Lord's Prayer is most perfect because it teaches us not only to ask for what we can rightly desire, but also in the order in which we should desire them."

Thomas Aquinas

"When you pray, move beyond words, and seek the heart behind them. The Lord's Prayer is not a ritual, but an invitation to daily communion with God."

John Wesley

"We can use no better words than the words which came from the lips of Him who 'spoke as never a man has spoken.'"

Charles Spurgeon

> *"The Lord's Prayer is not merely the pattern prayer, but the way we enter into Jesus' own prayer life, into His intimacy with the Father."*
>
> Dietrich Bonhoeffer

> *"The Lord's Prayer correctly understood is one of the high roads into the central mystery of Christian salvation and Christian experience."*
>
> N.T. Wright

And finally, this last quote I find one of the most insightful. It highlights how the Lord's Prayer is not just meant to be mindlessly recited. It's to be used as a structure or a guide for an entire session of prayer.

> *"To cultivate a deeper prayer life all you have to do is say the Lord's Prayer - but take an hour to do it."*
>
> Timothy Jones

Is it possible that the Lord's Prayer holds a power and a purpose that many of us have not yet tapped into? I believe the answer is yes.

Peter the Barber and Luther's Gift of a Prayer Guide

Martin Luther was one of the most influential men in church history. His boldness confronting the darkness and heresy within the Roman Catholic led to the protestant reformation. His close friend, Veit Dietrich, once wrote about Luther's personal prayer life:

INTRODUCTION

> *"There is not a day on which he does not devote at least three hours, the very ones most suitable for work, to prayer. Once I was fortunate to overhear his prayer. Good God, what faith in his words! He speaks with the great reverence of one who speaks to his God, and with the trust and hope of one who speaks with his father and friend."*
>
> Veit Dietrich (friend of Martin Luther)

Where did this powerful and rich prayer life come from? We can see a glimpse in some of his writings.

When Martin Luther's barber, Peter, asked for help learning to pray, Luther wrote him a letter that was later converted to a little book called, *A Simple Way to Pray*. Peter later faced exile after a tragic accident, but he took Luther's letter with him, practicing its simple structure for the rest of his life.

What did Luther recommend? The essence of what Luther taught Peter could be summarised in three simple principles:

1. Make prayer a daily discipline.

Set aside time each day before distractions begin, as an intentional act of devotion. Luther's pattern was to pray morning and night using the Lord's Prayer, inserting his own needs into each line.

2. Let the Lord's Prayer guide you.

Use each line of Jesus' great prayer as a launching pad – paraphrasing, reflecting, and personalising it in your own words.

3. Follow the Spirit's leading.

After praying through the structure of the Lord's Prayer, bring before God anything else on your heart, allowing the Holy Spirit to guide you.

If followed, these principles can revolutionise your prayer life.

But let's be honest. Some days prayer flows from our hearts easily; other days it feels like a slog. But if prayer becomes a habit, we continue regardless of feelings.

Praying with Clarity and Focus

If you're anything like me, one of the greatest challenges in prayer is avoiding distraction. I can be praying through my list, then suddenly remember something urgent and think, *"Oh, that will only take two minutes..."* And before I know it, half an hour has gone by and I'm saying, *"Oh, sorry Lord, I completely forgot You were there."*

But using the Lord's Prayer helps me remain more emotionally and mentally engaged. It tends to anchor me and keep me engaged.

In the following chapters, we'll walk through each verse of the Lord's Prayer, unpacking its meaning and learning how to pray through it daily.

Before We Begin: An Overview of the Lord's Prayer

Although I've structured this book with one verse of the Lord's Prayer per chapter, Jesus actually models for us nine different prayer points:

Chapter 1 (Matthew 6:9):
1. **Adoration** – *"Our Father in heaven"*
2. **Worship** – *"Hallowed be your name"*

Chapter 2 (Matthew 6:10):
3. **Mission** – *"Your kingdom come, your will be done..."*

Chapter 3 (Matthew 6:11):
4. **Provision** – *"Give us today our daily bread"*

Chapter 4 (Matthew 6:12):
5. **Confession** – *"Forgive us our debts"*
6. **Forgiveness** – *"As we forgive our debtors"*

Chapter 5 (Matthew 6:13):
7. **Freedom** – *"Lead us not into temptation"*
8. **Deliverance** – *"Deliver us from the evil one"*

Chapter 6 (a later manuscript addendum to Matthew 6:13):
9. **Praise** – *"Yours is the kingdom, power, and glory"*

Finally, Chapter 7 concludes with some practical insights on how to get started with your own daily discipline of prayer.

Take note - each chapter ends with some reflection questions and a sample prayer. I hope this will help you more effectively apply what Jesus is teaching us.

Prayer is More Than a Crisis Line

One final thought before we get into the first chapter... Jesus wants to challenge us beyond the default way that most people pray.

Before surrendering to Christ, or in the early stages of faith, many people only pray in response to a crisis - when jobs are threatened, money is tight, or when relationships are falling apart. Of course, God welcomes those prayers.

In fact, *Psalm 50:15* says: *"Call upon me in the day of trouble; I will deliver you, and you shall glorify me."*

But Jesus wants to lead us further still into a higher motivation – into a kind of prayer that's not driven by crisis. He wants to draw us into desire for Him – a life of prayer where God Himself is our reward.

Jesus is inviting us into His relationship with the Father - into a communion where the Father becomes our happiness.

The Lord's Prayer is Jesus' invitation into His own intimacy with the Father.

And so, in the chapters that follow, we'll walk line by line through Christ's extraordinary prayer.

Let's not approach it as a ritual, but as an invitation into relationship. Not as formula, but as the formation of our souls into a loving union with God.

It's time to learn to pray – *not like the hypocrites, not like the pagans,* but as sons and daughters of God.

Chapter One
First Things First
Prayers of Adoration and Worship

As I mentioned before, I've been a follower of Jesus for nearly 30 years. But it's probably only in the last ten years that I've become consistently mindful of the importance of adoration and worship in my personal prayer.

That means for the first twenty years of my Christian life, most of my prayer time focused on the other parts of the Lord's Prayer – asking for provision, forgiveness, guidance, and protection, or perhaps declaring God's Word over my future. I largely ignored or skipped over the very first line of the Lord's Prayer.

Of course, I would worship God through songs at church or occasionally on my own, and I'm sure I prayed at least a few prayers of adoration during those years. But I can't recall it ever being a normal or intentional part of the way that I approached God.

At best, I felt a vague obligation to begin with some words of thanksgiving or praise. Primarily because I had heard Psalm 100:4, which says, "Enter His gates with thanksgiving, and His courts with praise…"

In the very first verse of the Lord's Prayer, Jesus clarifies the highest goal of prayer:

> *Pray then like this: "Our Father in heaven, hallowed be your name.*
>
> Matthew 6:9 (ESV)

The Highest Goal of Prayer

The highest goal of prayer is an intimate relationship with God as Father.

When we begin to pray, the first thing on our minds shouldn't be our needs or our sins, but the simple and profound reality that we are children coming into the presence of a loving Father.

Of course, this can be challenging – because all of us have had different experiences with our earthly fathers. In a perfect world, every father would reflect the character and love of our heavenly Father. But we don't live in a perfect world.

If you did have a present and affectionate father, it might feel natural to relate to God in this way. But if you didn't, you may need to relearn what "Father" truly means.

Healing Father Wounds

I had a great relationship with my dad for many years, but things went down hill when I hit my teenage years. My parents divorced after my dad had several affairs and abandoned our home. It wounded me deeply and left me with many insecurities.

I've known others who had fathers who were angry or abusive. You may have had a dad who was a strong authority figure but was emotionally distant. Whether we've had "daddy issues" or not, we will all need our mind renewed in some way about what God is like as a Father.

When Jesus invites us to address God as Father, what does He mean?

Although the New Testament was written in Greek, Jesus didn't speak Greek to His disciples. First-century Jews primarily spoke Aramaic, and we find many Aramaic phrases scattered throughout the New Testament.

There were two different Aramaic words for "Father." One was *Avi*, which carried the weight of authority or origin – like calling Abraham the "father of many nations," or referring to someone as a "founding father."

But that's not the word Jesus used. When Jesus referred to God as Father, He used the word *Abba* – a word of deep familiarity and affection.

We see this in His prayer in the Garden of Gethsemane:

> *"And he said, 'Abba, Father, all things are possible for you. Remove this cup from me. Yet not what I will, but what you will.'"*
>
> Mark 14:36 (ESV)

The Jewish leaders in Jesus' day had no problem calling God their Father using formal language – but to call Him *Abba*? That was unthinkably personal. It was too familiar and even considered irreverent.

Abba is the equivalent of saying, "Daddy" or "Papa." It conveys not just authority, but warmth, affection, and trust.

I once heard a friend tell a story about being on a plane in the Middle East. A little boy was running down the aisle with his arms lifted high, calling out, "Abba! Abba!" – as if to say, "Pick me up, Daddy." That's the heart behind the word that Jesus used when addressing God.

And this is how Jesus calls us to approach God – with childlike love and trust.

> *"For you did not receive the spirit of slavery to fall back into fear, but you have received the Spirit of adoption as sons, by whom we cry, 'Abba! Father!' The Spirit himself bears witness with our spirit that we are children of God."*
>
> Romans 8:15–16 (ESV)

Not everyone can call God *Abba*. He is only *Abba* to those who are in Christ – those who have been adopted into His family by faith. In Christ, we are given a new identity and status. We are called children of God.

And with that status comes privilege – the privilege of bold access to God and the promise of an inheritance.

Sons Ask Differently

Earlier, I referred to the photo of JFK's son playing under the President's desk in the Oval Office. No other child in the country could play in such a privileged area. JFK was president to the nation, but only *Abba* to his son.

In the very first line of the Lord's Prayer, Jesus is telling us that this is the kind of access we now have in heaven.

So, when you pray, begin with a celebration of this intimacy with God. Begin with adoration, coming as a son or daughter who knows they are loved.

And come to Him mindful of your rights – knowing you have an inheritance.

Imagine if my son Ben and his friend both came to me separately and asked me for money. Who do you think would have a better chance of getting what they requested? Of course, my own son.

Now imagine they both go and ask the friend's dad for money. It's a different outcome altogether.

Why? Because sons make requests to their fathers with the confidence of an heir.

This is the kind of boldness Jesus gives us through His own relationship with the Father. We are welcomed into the same intimacy and boldness in prayer that Jesus experienced. We are to celebrate this when we pray.

Adoration Means Enjoying the Father's Presence

So, in our times of prayer, Jesus says to begin by adoring who God is as our Father. We don't rush into our list of needs – we simply come and enjoy Him.

When we say, "Our Father," we're recognizing that we belong to God and He belongs to us. We're acknowledging our identity as heirs.

Sometimes my kids will come into my office while I'm working just because they want to talk to me – not because they want anything, but because they love their dad, and they know I love them. They don't care if they're disturbing me. They enjoy my presence and know that I enjoy theirs.

That's adoration.

Worshipping in the Light of God's Holiness

Verse 9 doesn't stop with, *"Our Father in heaven."* It continues: *"Hallowed be your name."*

Here, with the knowledge of our sonship already firmly established in our hearts, Jesus invites us to worship the Father in the light of His holiness.

Knowing God as Father stirs love and trust. But seeing God as holy stirs awe and reverence.

This is exactly what Jesus calls us to do next in prayer. He tells us to pause – whether for a brief moment or longer – and meditate on the holiness of God. Then, like the angels around His throne, we declare what we see back to Him in worshipful reverence and awe.

What Does It Mean to Say That God Is Holy?

To *hallow* something is to treat it as sacred, to honour it as set apart. The word *holy* means two things:

God's Holiness Refers to His Transcendence

This means God is completely "other" – utterly distinct from His creation. He is outside of time and space. He is infinite, eternal, and unchangeable. He exists above, beyond, and apart from everything He has made.

We begin to grasp this when we ponder the vastness of the universe. Think about what we see in the Hubble or James Webb telescopes. Maybe you've watched the video on YouTube that compares the sizes of stars. It shows a stream of comparisons, each star exponentially bigger than the last – and all unfathomably huge.

Even just considering the closest star to our sun, we find it is more than four light-years away. That means the light we see from that star today took four years to travel to us.

Keep in mind that, as far as we are from our own sun, that light only takes eight minutes and twenty seconds to reach us.

If we were to travel to our closest star, four light years away, if we could travel at 700,000 km/h (the speed of our fastest rocket), it would take over 6,500 years to get there.

The vastness of the universe reveals something to us about what God is like.

> *"The heavens declare the glory of God, and the sky above proclaims his handiwork."*
>
> Psalm 19:1 (ESV)

When we consider the scope of God's creation, we get a glimpse of His transcendence. He is unfathomably big and incomparably great. If we can't even fully comprehend the universe He made, how much greater is He?

God's Holiness Refers to His Moral Perfection

God is not only transcendent – He is also perfectly pure. There is no sin in Him. In fact, He Himself defines what is good and right by His very nature.

Sin is sin precisely because it is unlike God.

And because God's character and nature is the definition of moral perfection, He cannot allow sin in His presence. Sin cannot coexist with God.

This is why Christ's sacrifice was necessary. Our sin separated us from God because He is holy. But Jesus removed that separation by taking away our sin and making us holy in His sight.

Adoration Purifies Motive

Of course, there's a difference between our positional holiness and the experience of how we live. But consistent prayers of adoration and worship help to purify the heart.

Jesus is very intentional with the order of the Lord's Prayer because He knows the problem we all face – being overly self-focused.

Most of our prompts to pray come from our own personal needs, desires, or times of crisis.

Often, these desperate requests for help from God will come out of our mouths even before we are saved. I remember once, before I was following Christ, I cried out to God in the middle of a bad acid trip. I was panicking, thinking I had killed my friend, who was also having a bad trip and had passed out on the bed, curled up in the foetal position. God graciously answered and miraculously made both of us instantly sober.

I was amazed and felt very grateful in the moment, but nothing changed in my life because I didn't desire God. I simply desired access to His power. Once He solved my problem, I was back to escaping from my insecurities through drugs.

God is gracious, and He will meet us in our pain, even when He knows our motives are impure. But Jesus wants to lead us into a better way of living.

Jesus gave us the Lord's Prayer in this specific order to retrain our instincts. He wants to prompt us daily to come before God not with a list of self-centred requests, but first with adoration and worship.

He's happy for us to bring our personal needs before the Father – but not to do so first. Before anything else, He wants our God-centred devotions. He seeks to dethrone the idols that try to take first place in our hearts.

Augustine and the Reordering of Disordered Loves

If we're honest, many of our requests to God – even good ones – are often subconsciously aimed at gaining more control, more comfort, or the approval of others. These are some of the most common idols in the human heart.

Starting prayer with adoration and worship focuses our attention on God Himself, not just what God can do for us. It anchors our hearts in who He is – our loving Father and our holy King – and reminds us that He should be our heart's greatest treasure.

Augustine, the early church father, didn't write much about prayer. But in one letter to a noblewoman in his church, he offered some profound wisdom on how to pray.

Before we can pray rightly, Augustine says, we must become a certain kind of person - one who realizes that no matter how much we possess in this life, those things will never bring lasting peace and joy. His advice is to, *"account yourself desolate in this world."*

That's a powerful phrase. It means we must come to terms with the fact that everything in this world – wealth, success, approval, and comfort – will ultimately leave us empty if they take God's place in our hearts. They can never meet our deepest needs and desires.

Augustine then speaks of what he calls *disordered loves.* That is, we often love certain things first when they should be loved third or fourth. This misalignment reveals our deepest battle.

We might say with our lips that our relationship with God is our highest priority and that His Kingdom is our greatest cause. But is His presence as experientially valuable to us as our comfort, our success, or our reputation?

Have you ever caught yourself thinking, *"If I just had _____ , all my problems would go away"?* Whatever is in that blank is probably an idol.

I've thought about this when I've considered what it must have been like to be Steve Jobs when he had a terminal cancer diagnosis. How frustrating must it have been to have billions of dollars and yet face a problem that money couldn't solve.

When we're confronted with our human frailty, we see more clearly that without God, we have nothing. Praying the Lord's Prayer daily helps to align our hearts with this truth – to reorder our loves in a way that reflects what is ultimately most important and experientially more satisfying.

The Secret of Friendship with God

The greatest reward of this reordering of our loves is deeper friendship with God.

This line, *"Hallowed be your name,"* is not only a declaration of truth but a confession of desire. We're not only affirming that God is holy – we're asking that His name would be treated as holy in our lives. We're inviting Him to purify our hearts.

The NLT pulls this idea out of the Greek with the translation, *"May your name be kept holy."*

This is a yearning for experiential holiness in our lives. This prayer communicates our desire to live in a way that will position us to enjoy God's presence more deeply.

You might think that pondering God's holiness would make us feel unworthy of calling Him "Father." But the opposite is true. A growing revelation of His holiness will deepen our intimacy with Him. It heightens our appreciation for Christ's finished work and leads us into greater closeness with Him.

David highlights this when he says,

> *"The friendship [secret counsel] of the Lord is for those who fear him, and he makes known to them his covenant."*
>
> Psalm 25:14 (ESV)

What a beautiful promise. Those who fear God are invited into deeper friendship and are shown more of the hidden blessings of the covenant promises we have in Him.

Here's another translation of the same verse:

> *"The Lord confides in those who fear him; he makes his covenant known to them."*
>
> Psalm 25:14 (NIV)

Ponder that thought: our fear of the Lord positions us to be someone in whom God confides. The more we fear Him, the more He feels that He can trust us.

Jesus wants us to enjoy this depth of intimate friendship with the Father. That's why He tells us to start all our times of prayer like this. Adoration and worship get our eyes off ourselves and onto God. They help us grow both in the knowledge of who we are as His children, and in our understanding of His holiness.

As we pray like this daily, we don't just know about God – we grow to know Him deeply and intimately. This kind of prayer opens our hearts to the kind of relationship with God where we're not just asking for things – we're encountering Him. He Himself becomes our reward.

You Have More Than You Think

Through daily adoration and worship, when we tell God again and again that nothing is more important than knowing Him, something begins to change in us. Our hearts are gradually delivered from idols, and we fall more and more into deep communion with Him.

We are slowly healed of our tendency to overvalue the wrong things, and the fear of the Lord positions us to be near to His heart.

This prioritising of God above all else is the only thing that can empower us to pray consistently. It's only when our greatest desire is God Himself that prayer becomes a joy and a delight rather than a chore and a duty.

If we only pray because we want something from God, then we will only pray when we feel desperate. And we don't feel desperate every day – because not every day do we feel threatened to lose something that we hold dear.

But if knowing God more and more each day is our highest treasure, then we will pray every day, no matter our circumstances – whether good or bad.

Reflection Questions for Chapter 1

1. When you think of God as "Father," what emotions, memories, or assumptions come up in your heart?

2. How might your earthly experience of fatherhood impact your ability to draw near to God in prayer?

3. Do you find it easier to approach God in prayer with your needs than with worship? Why do you think that is?

4. When was the last time you paused simply to adore God—not for what He gives, but for who He is?

5. What "disordered loves" might be competing with your desire for God Himself?

6. In what ways could starting your prayers with worship help realign your heart?

7. How might meditating on God's transcendence and holiness change the way you view your daily struggles or desires?

A Prayer of Adoration and Worship

Our Father in heaven, hallowed be your name...

Father, I come to You not as a stranger or a servant, but as Your beloved child. Thank You for adopting me into Your family through Jesus. You are not distant or cold. You are near, tender, and full of mercy.

And yet, You are also holy – set apart in Your majesty, beauty, and power. There is no one like You in heaven or on earth. You are infinite in wisdom, eternal in strength, and perfect in righteousness.

Let Your name be treated as holy in my life today. Let the way I speak, think, and act reflect my awe of who You are. Guard my heart from casual familiarity. Help me never forget the wonder of having full access to Your presence.

I worship You – not for what You can do for me, but simply because of who You are.

Be glorified in my life today.

Chapter Two

Prioritising God's Desires

Kingdom-Centred Missional Prayers

In the last chapter, we talked about reordering the loves of the heart so that God remains most important. But the beginning of the Lord's Prayer not only reveals that the Father should have the highest place in our hearts. It also teaches us that His Kingdom should have the second-highest place.

The Already, But Not Yet Kingdom

Not long after I became a Christian during my time at university, I attended a midweek service where a guest prophet from Wales was ministering. At one point in the evening, he called me out and shared a prophetic word over my life. I don't recall all the details of what he said – but I do remember the feeling his words left me with.

For the first time in my life, I felt like I had a reason for existing that was bigger than my own comfort or pleasure. That word sparked something in me – a vision for a grand purpose that stretched well beyond my life and any personal concerns.

That prophetic word was, in hindsight, the seed of a Kingdom vision that transformed my reason for existing.

As that vision grew, it began to rewire how I saw everything. Where once I felt mostly hopeless about the future of the world, I now found myself filled with an unshakeable sense of hope: the future could be different – and, somehow, I was invited into God's plan to make it so.

In the Lord's Prayer, Jesus seeks to awaken daily in every believer a strong Kingdom vision. He does this by teaching us to prioritise prayers for the coming of His Kingdom:

> *"Your kingdom come, Your will be done, on earth as it is in heaven."*
>
> Matthew 6:10 (ESV)

This prayer is more than an idealistic wish – it's a call to align our desires and will with the very purpose and will of God.

After Jesus rose from the dead but before He ascended to heaven, He spent 40 days teaching His disciples about one thing: the Kingdom of God. He knew that He was about to hand over to the Church the most important mission to ever exist – the restoration of all things – and He needed His leaders to see what He saw.

So, what is the Kingdom of God?

Let's attempt to answer that question by looking at a few quotes from some well-known theologians and pastors:

"The Kingdom is primarily the dynamic reign or kingly rule of God; and derivatively, the sphere in which that rule is experienced."

George Eldon Ladd:

"The Kingdom of God is the range of God's effective will – where what God wants done is done."

Dallas Willard

N.T. Wright echoes this sentiment:

"The Kingdom of God is what it looks like when God is running the show."

N.T. Wright

"The Kingdom of God is the reign of God manifested in Christ to bring redemption to His people and to establish justice and peace among the nations of the earth."

Anthony Hoekema

"The Kingdom is the renewed order of things, the great restoration of all that had been corrupted by sin."

Herman Ridderbos

At the heart of each of these definitions is the same basic idea: the Kingdom of God on earth is His rule manifest in the hearts of people and in the places where those people gain influence.

In heaven exists the full expression of the reality of God's Kingdom. There, God's will is done joyfully and perfectly. There's no resistance, no rebellion, no death, no sickness, and no sin.

When we pray, *"Your kingdom come,"* we're asking for that same reality to be increasingly manifest on the earth – in our hearts, our families, our churches, our cities, and the nations of the world.

Jesus said the Kingdom of God has already come, but He also said it has not yet fully come. It's already here – and yet, it's not fully here.

> *"...the kingdom of God is in the midst of you."*
> Luke 17:21 (ESV)

Kingdom power has already broken in. But the fullness is still to come. That's why, later, Jesus speaks of drinking wine again only *"when the kingdom of God comes"* (Luke 22:18).

This is the great tension we live in: the Kingdom has come, but it has not yet fully come.

And this is why we, as the people of God, must pray Kingdom-centred prayers. It's through both our prayers and our obedience that God's Kingdom comes in greater measure.

Praying God's Desires

When Jesus taught us to pray, *"Your kingdom come, your will be done on earth as it is in heaven,"* He wasn't giving us a poetic way to open our prayers. He was handing us an assignment.

As we said in the last chapter, most of our prayers tend to revolve around our own lives:

"God, help me with this big decision."

"Bless my finances."

"Protect my family."

None of that is wrong. These are all good things to pray. In fact, Jesus welcomes prayers for our personal needs later in the Lord's Prayer when he prays, *"Give us this day our daily bread..."*

But before we ask for our personal needs and desires, He invites us to prioritise requests that align with His greatest desires.

He says, before we ask for anything else, to pray for His Kingdom to come – to pray for God's rule to expand into every place that currently resists it.

God's Kingdom Comes First in the Heart

When we pray, *"Your kingdom come,"* we're not just asking for something to happen around us – we're inviting something to happen first within us.

The coming of the Kingdom is ultimately a confrontation with human will. It asks a fundamental question: Who's in charge here? Who's the King?

That's why Jesus launched His ministry with this announcement:

> *"Now after John was arrested, Jesus came into Galilee, proclaiming the gospel of God, and saying, 'The time is fulfilled, and the kingdom of God is at hand; repent and believe in the gospel.'"*
>
> Mark 1:14–15 (ESV)

The Kingdom of God begins to break in when a person repents and believes, turning from self-rule and sin, and surrendering to Jesus as Lord.

In fact, a person can only enter God's Kingdom through a complete spiritual rebirth. Jesus explains this to Nicodemus in John 3:

> *"Truly, truly, I say to you, unless one is born again, he cannot see the kingdom of God."*
>
> John 3:3 (ESV)

This kind of transformation is not "cosmetic." It's not about improving behaviour, looking better on the outside, or trying harder to be good. It's a total change of heart that can only be accomplished in us by God. As Paul says:

> *"He has delivered us from the domain of darkness and transferred us to the kingdom of his beloved Son, in whom we have redemption, the forgiveness of sins."*
>
> Colossians 1:13–14 (ESV)

We can't strive our way into the Kingdom – we must be transferred into His Kingdom by grace. And one of the marks of this grace at work in our lives is a growing desire to do God's will.

So, the first human will to be confronted when praying the Lord's Prayer is our own.

> *For the grace of God has appeared, bringing salvation for all people, training us to renounce ungodliness and*

> *worldly passions... to purify for himself a people... zealous for good works.*
>
> Titus 2:11–14 (ESV)

Before we pray for God's Kingdom to come to the world, we should pray that God's Kingdom comes more fully to our own hearts – that we would surrender more deeply to His will.

First in the Heart, Then on the Earth

Jesus taught that the Kingdom would grow progressively – slowly and silently – like a small seed transforming into a large tree and like leaven working its way through dough.

> *"The kingdom of heaven is like a grain of mustard seed... It is the smallest of all seeds, but when it has grown it is larger than all the garden plants... The kingdom of heaven is like leaven that a woman took and hid in three measures of flour, till it was all leavened."*
>
> Matthew 13:31–33 (ESV)

This is how the Kingdom has spread over the past 2,000 years – not through instant revolutions, but through multi-generational, faithful obedience. It starts small, but over millennia, it will transform the entire world.

This long-term view of the progressive growth of God's Kingdom should inform everything in our lives, especially how we pray.

In fact, the most fundamental evidence that we desire what God desires is our commitment to persevere in praying Kingdom-centred prayers. We should not just offer up vague hopes, but specific, targeted, Scripture-based prayers that align with the mission of God.

Let's explore how to pray these Kingdom-centred prayers.

Prayers That Bring God's Kingdom

When Jesus taught us to pray, *"Your kingdom come, your will be done, on earth as it is in heaven,"* He was inviting us to participate in the invasion of His rule into the world.

He calls us to pray prayers that shake the powers of darkness, transform people from the inside out, and even renew culture for His glory.

Below are seven simple, potent, and biblically grounded Kingdom prayers you can incorporate into your own times of prayer:

1. Dethrone Every Idol in My Own Heart

> *"Search me, O God, and know my heart..."*
> Psalm 139:23 (ESV)

Before we pray for the Kingdom to come around us, we must first welcome it within us. The first battleground of the Kingdom is our own hearts. Every day we are tempted to enthrone lesser gods – comfort, control, approval, power, sex, money. We begin with our own surrender.

These prayers might sound like:
- "Jesus, reign in me. Dethrone every idol. Reorder my loves."

- "Let Your Kingdom come to my inner world - my thoughts, affections, and motives."

The Kingdom expands through the holiness of His people. As Christ reigns in our hearts, His Kingdom flows through our lives.

2. Send Revival to My City and Nation

> *Will you not revive us again, that your people may rejoice in you? Show us your steadfast love, O Lord, and grant us your salvation.*
>
> Psalm 85:6–7 (ESV)

Revival is what it looks like when God's Kingdom breaks in with power and the glory of His presence. For God's Kingdom to come, we need the Holy Spirit to awaken hearts, transform culture, and make people in every sphere of society aware of His presence.

These prayers might sound like:
- "Lord, reveal Yourself to the people of our city."
- "Let the fear of the Lord return to the Church."
- "Stir repentance, holiness, hunger, and worship in our city."

3. Soften the Hearts of Leaders, That the Gospel Would Spread Freely

> *"Pray... for kings and all who are in high positions..."*

1 Timothy 2:1–4 (ESV)

We don't just vote or critique government leaders – we intercede for them. Scripture commands us to pray for those in authority, so that the gospel can advance as the society flourishes in peace. Good civil leadership creates space for Kingdom expansion.

These prayers might sound like:

- "Father, give our civil leaders wisdom, restraint, and courage to govern justly."

- "May laws be passed that protect life, freedom, and the spread of the gospel."

- "Soften hearts in government – open doors so the gospel can be proclaimed in our halls of parliament."

4. Save My Lost Friends and Family

"The Lord... is patient... not wishing that any should perish..."

2 Peter 3:9 (ESV)

Jesus came to seek and save the lost. As we pray for the Kingdom to come, we should pray for individual hearts to be born again. This is where Kingdom work becomes personal.

These prayers might sound like:

- "Lord, open their eyes to see you. Soften their hearts to believe."

- "Convict them of sin and reveal Jesus as Lord and Saviour."

- "Put people in their path to share the gospel. Speak to them through dreams, visions, and special messengers."

One important discipline here is to keep an "Impact List" – names of friends, family, and co-workers who are far from God – and pray for them by name daily. Their salvation will be a powerful sign that the Kingdom is breaking through by your life and prayers.

5. Strengthen the Church

> *"Sanctify them in the truth... As You sent me, I send them."*
>
> John 17:17–18 (ESV)

The Church is the outpost of the Kingdom on earth. When the local church is strong – spiritually, doctrinally, and relationally – the Kingdom advances. Jesus prayed for our sanctification, our unity, and our mission. We should do the same.

These prayers might sound like:

- "Refine Your Church, Lord. Purify our hearts and teaching."

- "Unite Your people. Heal division. Bind us together in love."

- "Fill us with boldness to preach, pray, and make disciples."

6. Send Out Labourers

> *"The harvest is plentiful, but the labourers are few..."*
> Matthew 9:37–38 (ESV)

Jesus didn't tell us to pray for the harvest. He said it's already ripe – what we need is more labourers. This is a prayer for multiplication – for workers in schools, businesses, politics, families, and the nations.

These prayers might sound like:

- "Lord, raise up more disciple-makers, missionaries, and five-fold ministers."

- "Call out the next generation of Kingdom leaders. Give them a vision for the growth of your Kingdom. Send them out into the harvest."

- "Multiply Kingdom leaders in every sphere – business, education, media, and government."

And as you pray this, don't just ask God to send others – ask him to send you!

7. Send Me and Use Me Today

> *"Here I am! Send me."*
> Isaiah 6:8 (ESV)

This is the most dangerous, but also the most glorious prayer we can pray. We are the answer to someone else's prayer. When we offer ourselves daily, the Kingdom moves through us.

These prayers might sound like:
- "Lord, send me today. Lead me into divine appointments to share Jesus."
- "Empower me with boldness, kindness, and courage."
- "Use me to bring the reality of who You are into every conversation today."

Don't wait for a "calling." If you are a disciple, you've already been commissioned to go.

Reflection Questions for Chapter 2

1. When you pray *"Your kingdom come,"* what comes to mind? Has this prayer become a routine phrase, or is it a daily alignment with God's mission?

2. Which of the seven areas of Kingdom prayer feels most natural for you? Which one challenges you?

3. Do you regularly pray for your national and local leaders? How might praying for government — rather than complaining about it — shift your perspective?

4. Do you pray for the lost by name? Who in your life needs to be transferred from the domain of darkness into the Kingdom of the beloved Son?

5. What would it look like for your prayer life to reflect multi-generational faith and long-term Kingdom vision?

6. Are you currently praying for more workers in God's harvest

field — including asking God to use you?

Kingdom-Centred Prayers

1. Dethrone Every Idol in My Own Heart

Father, before I pray for the world around me, I ask that Your Kingdom would come in me. Search my heart. Expose anything I've put above You – anything I rely on more than Your grace. Dismantle the idols of comfort, control, and approval. Jesus, be enthroned again in my thoughts, my priorities, and my desires. Let Your will be done in me as it is in heaven.

2. Send Revival to My City and Nation

Lord, open the heavens and come down. Revive Your Church and awaken this city. Let the fear of the Lord return to our land. Let righteousness be loved again. Stir hunger for You in the hearts of Your people and draw those far from You into the light of Your truth. Move with power in families, schools, and workplaces. Let this generation see Your glory.

3. Soften the Hearts of Our Government Leaders

God of all wisdom, we lift up those who govern, both locally and nationally. Guide them in righteousness. Restrain corruption. Give them courage to do what is right. Create space for the gospel to spread. Let freedom be protected. May the laws of our land honour Your ways and make room for Your Word to spread.

4. Save My Lost Friends and Family

Jesus, You came to seek and save the lost – and I lift up to You those I love who are far from You. Break the hardness in their hearts. Open their minds to the truth. Let the gospel shine like light in the darkness. Holy Spirit, convict them of sin, reveal the beauty of the gospel, and draw them into the Kingdom of Your Son.

5. Strengthen the Church

Father, strengthen Your Church. Purify our hearts. Unite us. Clarify our mission. Let us walk in holiness and truth, with love that reflects who You are and what You're like. Fill us with boldness to preach the gospel, to stand for righteousness, and to disciple the next generation of leaders. Cause Your Body to rise in maturity, courage, and compassion.

6. Send Out Labourers

Lord of the harvest, the fields are ready – so send more workers. Call missionaries, church planters, and five-fold ministers to serve You. Make every Christian a disciple-maker. Raise up leaders in every sphere – government, business, media, medicine, education. Empower Your people to go with faith, love, and power. Multiply the labourers. Increase our impact.

7. Send Me and Use Me Today

Here I am, Lord – send me. Use me today as Your ambassador. Let my words carry grace and truth. Help me to see the opportunities You've placed in my path. Use my life today to point lost people to Jesus. I give You my hands, my voice, and my time. Let Your Kingdom come through me today.

Chapter Three

Looking to God as Provider

Prayers for Personal Provision

Let's read the Lord's Prayer again, with special attention on verse 11. Remember, this prayer was Jesus' response to the disciples' request: "Lord, teach us to pray."

As we've already seen, His model prayer was not a formula or an incantation to be mindlessly memorised, but a framework for how to approach God in prayer.

Let's read it again as a whole.

> *⁹ Pray then like this:*
> *"Our Father in heaven,*
> *hallowed be your name.*
> *¹⁰ Your kingdom come,*
> *your will be done,*

> *on earth as it is in heaven.*
> *[11] Give us this day our daily bread,*
> *[12] and forgive us our debts,*
> *as we also have forgiven our debtors.*
> *[13] And lead us not into temptation,*
> *but deliver us from evil.*
>
> Matthew 6:9–13 (ESV)

The structure of the Lord's Prayer teaches us how to pray from the heart. Each phrase is like a bullet point, guiding us in how to pray and what to pray for.

As we've already covered:

"Our Father in heaven" draws us into intimacy and reorients us as God's beloved children.

"Hallowed be your name" calls us into reverent worship, remembering that our Father is also the Holy Creator of the universe.

"Your kingdom come" then leads us to pray bold, Kingdom-centred prayers for revival, salvation, discipleship, and cultural transformation – prayers that move the proverbial ball down the field of God's redemptive purpose, so to speak.

And then, only after all this, we arrive at verse 11:

> *"Give us this day our daily bread."*
>
> Matthew 6:11 (ESV)

Putting Needs in Their Proper Place

LOOKING TO GOD AS PROVIDER

Why does Jesus place our personal needs fourth in the list of what to pray? The answer can only be that He wants to reorder our priorities.

We highlighted this in the last chapter but think again about when most of us tend to pray. It's often only in crisis, when we're desperate, anxious, and out of options. And what do we pray about? Whatever it is that we feel we desperately need.

But Jesus doesn't call us to begin there. He places prayers for our personal needs after adoration, worship, and Kingdom-centred intercession. Why?

Because God is not a genie. He is our Father. He desires for us to connect with Him relationally and to worship Him considering who He is, all before we petition Him.

And then, when we do petition Him, He wants our hearts to care most about what He cares about, trusting that as we "seek first the Kingdom," all our other needs and desires will be taken care of.

God wants to meet our needs, but He wants us to know that our needs are already met in Him. The prayer – and consistently praying it – teaches us to approach God not as the one who gives us what we want, but as the One who should be who we want most.

Once our hearts are rightly aligned with God, we are safely positioned to receive from Him. Only when God has become our greatest desire can He trust us with the good, temporal gifts He wants to give us.

Aligned Hearts Can Freely Ask

Jesus said:

> *"If you abide in me, and my words abide in you, ask whatever you wish, and it will be done for you."*

John 15:7 (ESV)

Notice, He doesn't say, *"Ask only for what you need, and nothing more."* No, He says *"whatever you wish."*

That's carte blanche access – but it's contingent upon abiding in Him. The more our hearts and desires are aligned with God's heart and His will, the more confident we will be in bringing our personal requests before Him.

I'm sure you have your own stories of how God has supernaturally provided for you, but let me share a few of my own experiences of God's abundant provision.

One of the first financial miracles I experienced was when I was 23 years old, about two years after I began to follow Christ.

I had just graduated from university and decided to commit the next year to a nine-month ministry and leadership training program at a related church in another city. While I wasn't certain that God had called me into vocational ministry – or even what that might look like – I knew I needed to take a year to seek the Lord before going into my planned career as a stockbroker.

I had practically no money in the bank, but I signed up for the program and hopped in my car to drive the five hours from my hometown of Memphis to St. Louis, Missouri. The semester began in August, and I was told I needed to pay around $400 per month to cover the cost of attending the college.

Fast forward to the end of November. God was moving powerfully in my life through the discipleship I was receiving, but I had not yet paid one cent toward my tuition. I was basically freeloading off the school and my host family.

As we approached the Thanksgiving holiday, I made plans to drive back to Memphis to visit my family. The dean of the school (who also happened to be the head teacher and the head of the host family I was living with) told me that unless I returned the next week with $800 cash, I shouldn't bother coming back!

I was desperate for a financial breakthrough or all my plans for the year would be dashed. Not only would that be an extremely crushing and embarrassing failure, but I knew God still had something for me in this year of training.

I had already been praying and declaring God's promises over my situation, but now my faith went into overdrive. I was staying up late and getting up early to seek God, declare His promises over my situation, and cry out to Him for His provision.

I enjoyed the weekend with my family, but then Sunday arrived, and it was time to prepare to head back to St. Louis. The only problem was that I still had no money, and I was told not to come back without a wad of cash.

So, I pack my bags in faith and drive to visit my home church on the Sunday morning before the drive back to St. Louis. I had no idea how, but I knew somehow that money was going to come to me.

Finally, after the service, at the eleventh hour, my phone rang. My Dad, who was working through his own financial challenges at the time, called to say, "Come meet me, I have $800 to give you." It was the exact amount I needed!

Over the next six months, God brought the remaining funds in to cover the costs of the training – most of it coming just in time. While I wouldn't recommend being as disorganised as I was in that season, God taught me important lessons about trusting Him for my personal needs.

As I was seeking Him and His Kingdom first, He was making sure I had all that I needed.

Little did I know these lessons of faith would be crucial in my next season.

At the end of that year, God called me to return to the *University of Memphis,* from where I had just graduated, to start an outreach sharing the gospel with students on campus.

My sending church didn't have the funds to pay my salary, so I started raising my own support from other Christians. Even though it was common in the States for domestic missionaries to invite other Christians to support them financially, it was one of the most challenging things I had ever done. I was completely unproven in ministry, and this process of raising support was way out of my comfort zone.

Because I was single at the time, my financial goal was a meagre $2000 per month. After months of consistent effort, meeting with other Christians, sharing my vision for reaching lost uni students, and asking for a monthly gift commitment, I had reached only half of my goal.

But every morning, I was declaring God's promises over my finances and crying out to Him to meet my needs.

Then, through a referral, I met a godly woman whose husband was a doctor. I shared my vision for seeing lost students saved and asked her to partner with me. Typically, I would ask for a monthly gift in the range of $50 to $100 per month. This time, I heard the Lord say, "Don't ask for a specific amount."

After inviting her to invest in my Kingdom work, she said, "Sure, I can help you reach your remaining goal by committing to $1000 per month." I tried not to look surprised and then sat and cried in my car, in awe of God's faithful provision.

Once again, God had come through powerfully for me. She and her husband became some of our most faithful ministry partners over the coming years, investing tens of thousands of dollars into our ministry.

God is always faithful to meet our personal needs as we persevere in prayers of faith.

How Jesus Disciples Us Through Our Needs

Here are five ways Jesus strengthens our dependence upon Him and increases our faith through the simple yet profound request: "*Give us this day our daily bread.*"

1. We must depend completely on God as our Provider.

Jesus says, "Give us this day our *daily* bread," not our weekly or annual bread. He calls us to trust Him for today, every day.

This metaphor of bread would have immediately reminded His disciples of Israel's journey through the wilderness and God's daily provision of manna.

You probably remember this Old Testament story: every morning, an edible substance they called "manna" appeared like dew on the ground. The people were to gather only what they needed for that day – except on the day before Sabbath, when they were permitted to gather enough for two days. On any other day, if they hoarded more than they needed, the leftovers would spoil with maggots.

Why would God do this? Because He was training them to rely on Him daily. He didn't want them to put their trust in stored-up provision, but in Him. This was a lesson in surrendering control and learning to rest in God's care.

In the same way, Jesus teaches us not to find our security in our savings, income, or assets – even though those are wise to steward. If our security is not found in God, we'll always be anxious, always striving, and never satisfied. "Enough" will always feel like "just a little bit more."

Sometimes, God allows us to go through lean seasons to teach us to trust Him. He desires to provide abundantly, but He requires that we cultivate faith in His promises.

Looking back, it was in my seasons of greatest need that I was most devoted to seeking God through His Word, standing on His promises. God didn't want me to stay in financial desperation, but He did want me to learn something from it.

2. We can trust God for our future needs.

There's an alternate translation of this "daily bread" prayer in the margin of the ESV: *"Give us today our bread for tomorrow."*

This reading of the Greek points to the one day in the week, the day before the Sabbath, when Israel was permitted to collect two days' worth of manna.

When considered from this perspective, we see that Jesus is not only inviting us to make requests for today, living daily in a posture of rest and trust, but also to look forward to the future with big dreams and goals.

Jesus Himself is our Sabbath rest. In Him, we can cease striving and resist anxious toil. We can pray for today's needs and tomorrow's provision with calm confidence, because in Christ, our future is secure.

We should therefore understand this verse is an invitation to pray not only for today's needs, but also for our long-term future financial goals. We can trust God with both.

God doesn't just care what we need today – He is concerned about what we'll need ten, twenty, or even fifty years from now. Whether that's education expenses, wedding costs, retirement needs, or an inheritance to leave to our children and grandchildren, God's foreknowledge and will extends far beyond these simple requests.

Go ahead and start bringing these long-term needs before the Lord even today.

3. Jesus leads us out of anxiety into restful trust.

When we pray daily for what we need, anxiety is pushed out by faith. Instead of waiting to pray until fear builds out of desperation, we bring our needs to God as they arise.

Right after teaching the Lord's Prayer, Jesus says repeatedly, "Do not be anxious." He illustrates this by pointing to the birds and the flowers:

"Look at the birds of the air... Consider the lilies of the field... Seek first the Kingdom... and all these things will be added to you." Matthew 6:25–34 (ESV)

God uses life's uncertainties – job insecurity, rising costs, unexpected setbacks – to disciple us. He's not just giving us provision; He's forming our hearts to fully trust Him.

Faith grows every time we respond to uncertainty by bringing our needs to the Father.

Rather than only doing this at the odd times that we feel desperate, He wants our prayers for personal provision to be a regular part of our daily prayers.

4. God calls us to diligence and hard work.

Sometimes, when I'm praying for provision, I hear God prompting me to act. Whether it's studying or training for a future role, seeking out work, running a business, or aiming for a promotion, there are often actions God calls us to take to align with the prayers He wants to answer.

Scripture affirms this:

> *"Lazy hands make for poverty, but diligent hands bring wealth."*
>
> Proverbs 10:4 (NIV)

And Paul was even more direct:

> *"If anyone is not willing to work, let him not eat."*
>
> 2 Thessalonians 3:10 (ESV)

God doesn't want spoiled children. He wants sons and daughters who take responsibility and learn to bear fruit.

Warren Buffet once said: "I want to give my kids just enough so that they feel like they can do anything, but not so much that they feel like doing nothing."

In the same way, God invites us into both faith and diligence. After all, faith without works is dead!

5. We should pray also for the needs of others.

Notice the plural: *"Give **us** this day our daily bread."*

The Lord's Prayer is communal. It trains us to lift others before God – not just ourselves.

When praying for daily bread, I often pause to pray through a list of people I know who are either in need or who have big goals – friends, family members, people in our church, entrepreneurs, and business leaders.

This habit builds compassion and keeps us from becoming spiritually self-absorbed.

When we pray for daily bread, Jesus is doing more than meeting our needs. He is shaping our hearts.

He teaches us to depend on the Father's provision, to trust Him with both present and future needs, to exchange anxiety for faith, to work diligently in partnership with Him, and to remember others in our prayers. In this simple request, our priorities are reordered, our trust is deepened, and our lives are trained to rest in God's care.

Reflection Questions for Chapter 3

1. In what areas of your life are you most tempted to rely on yourself rather than trust God for daily provision?

2. How have you seen God provide for you in the past? How does remembering those stories help you trust Him today?

3. What is one area of anxiety you can bring before God right now in prayer?

4. Are you able to receive God's provision with contentment, even when it doesn't look like abundance? Why or why not?

5. How is your work ethic connected to your prayer life? Is there an area where God might be calling you to act in response to your prayers?

6. Who in your life could you be praying for today who also needs God's provision?

A Prayer for Personal Provision

Father, thank You that You are my Provider. You faithfully meet every need. You've been so generous toward me in the past, and so I trust You with my needs today...

Help me to walk in faith, not fear, as I look to my future...

Help me to grow in contentment and show me how to be generous toward others who are also in need. More than food, I need to clearly hear Your voice. I live by every word that comes from Your mouth. Help me to work with diligence, pray with faith, and rest with confidence that You will supply all I need, and even more – today and in the future.

Chapter Four
Reconciliation with God and People
Receiving and Giving Forgiveness in Prayer

As we continue learning how Jesus teaches us to pray, we arrive at one of the most powerful and personally transformative parts of the Lord's Prayer:

> *"And forgive us our debts, as we also have forgiven our debtors."*
>
> Matthew 6:12 (ESV)

The *New Living Translation* reads "*sins*" instead of "*debts*":

> *"And forgive us our sins, as we have forgiven those who sin against us."*
>
> Matthew 6:12 (NLT)

Then, just two verses later, Jesus adds a confronting elaboration:

> *"For if you forgive others their trespasses, your heavenly Father will also forgive you, but if you do not forgive others their trespasses, neither will your Father forgive your trespasses."*
>
> Matthew 6:14–15 (ESV)

Wow, those are some very high stakes!

Jesus clearly considers this part of His prayer worthy of special attention. After the prayer finishes, He circles back to the importance of giving forgiveness to ensure we don't miss the gravity of what He's teaching.

In this part of the Lord's Prayer, Jesus invites us to practice two disciplines every single day:

1. Confess any known sin to God, asking Him for forgiveness.

2. Declare to God that we have forgiven those who have sinned against us.

Receiving Forgiveness is Healing for the Soul

Everyone who has started following Christ has a story of receiving God's forgiveness. Most of us have also walked the difficult road of offering forgiveness to others.

Sin always has a vertical and horizontal dimension. It affects our relationship with God, and it affects our relationships with people.

I became a Christian during my third year at university in 1995. One Sunday morning, alone in my bedroom, I prayed a simple prayer of commitment to Jesus. That moment changed everything about my life – new desires, new habits, new friends, and a new life purpose.

But one of the most dramatic changes I immediately experienced was in my ability to fall asleep. Up until that day, when I crawled into bed, I struggled with racing thoughts, anxiety, and an inability to rest. But that first night after committing my life to Jesus, I laid my head on the pillow and fell asleep immediately. No racing mind. No anxiety. Just rest.

Why? The only difference on day one was that I had received forgiveness from God. That experience taught me something profound: what I thought was a restless mind was actually a guilty conscience before God. Once I knew I was loved by God and truly forgiven – even for future sins I had not yet committed – a deep sense of peace rushed into my soul.

The Healing Power of Giving Forgiveness

Another major shift happened in my relationships. The hatred I held in my heart toward those who had done me wrong began to melt away.

My relationship with my father, who had deeply hurt me, started to heal. Though boundaries were still necessary, I found a new freedom to love him. Emotional wounds felt less painful. Forgiveness I received from God was now overflowing.

Forgiveness doesn't just heal the heart – it touches every part of us.

Dr. Michael Barry, author of *The Forgiveness Project*, found that more than 61% of cancer patients he surveyed had significant forgiveness issues. This suggests a real, measurable connection between emotional wounds and physical health.

Scripture affirms this link:

> *"A peaceful heart leads to a healthy body; jealousy is like cancer in the bones."*
>
> Proverbs 14:30 (NLT)

That word jealousy in Hebrew can also mean bitterness or anger. No wonder Jesus calls us to regularly receive and give forgiveness – it protects both our soul and our body.

Why Forgiveness Is So Difficult

Forgiveness, however, is not easy.

Before we ask God for forgiveness, we must humbly acknowledge our own sin. That's difficult for most people because the default mode of the human heart is pride. Pride makes it easy to see the sin in others but difficult to see the sin in us, especially sins of the mind or motives, which aren't as obvious as outward behaviour.

Our culture doesn't help us. It hates the idea of sin. What God calls sin; many today call identity. "I was born this way" has become a shield against moral accountability.

Time magazine printed an article back in 1994 titled, "Infidelity: It May Be in Our Genes." It examined the promiscuous mating patterns of baboons and suggested that, because humans share evolutionary ancestry with them, we too are biologically wired for unfaithfulness. The message was clear: sexual sin isn't really sin – it's just science.

This kind of worldview is appealing because it removes God from our field of view. If there is no God, then there is no one to ultimately be accountable to. If I'm just a product of my biology, then no one has a right to tell me how to live. I can feel justified in doing what is right in my own eyes.

But to confess sin is to acknowledge the opposite: there is a holy God before whom I will give an account. That perspective requires humility that flows from a revelation of the character and nature of God.

The First Sin Response: Hiding and Blaming

This struggle with confession goes all the way back to Eden.

When Adam and Eve feared accountability, they hid from God.

> *"They heard the sound of the Lord God walking in the garden... and the man and his wife hid themselves... And the Lord God called... 'Where are you? And he said, 'I was afraid... and I hid myself.'"*
>
> Genesis 3:8–10 (ESV)

Then comes the blame-game. Adam blamed his wife, and then Eve blamed the devil.

> *"Who told you that you were naked?" the Lord God asked. "Have you eaten from the tree whose fruit I commanded you not to eat?" The man replied, "It was the woman you gave me who gave me the fruit, and I ate it." Then the Lord God asked the woman, "What have you done?" The serpent deceived me," she replied. "That's why I ate it."*
>
> Genesis 3:11–13 (NLT)

They both hid. They both cast blame. They both avoided responsibility.

But Jesus calls us out of hiding. He calls us out of the blame game. He calls us to bring our sins into the light, remembering how He's already dealt with our sin on the cross.

Why Confession Comes Fifth in the Lord's Prayer

One of the surprising things about Jesus' prayer is the order in which He places the call to confess sin. It's surprisingly far down the list.

Instead, Jesus teaches us to:

- Adore God as Father

- Worship His holiness

- Offer Kingdom-centred petitions

- Ask for personal provision

Then, and only then... confess our sins.

That's striking because it reveals that God does not want us to live under a constant sin-consciousness. He invites us to freely come to Him as children who know they have free access to their Father.

But many Christians, including myself in the past, feel a need to start their prayers confessing all the bad things they've done since they last prayed. It's like we feel we need to clean ourselves up before God will listen, as if it's up to us to absolve ourselves of guilt before He will hear us.

But that couldn't be further from the truth. When we first come to God, He doesn't want us to talk about our sins. He wants us to enjoy Him as our merciful and compassionate Father. If we have trusted in

Christ to be made right with God, then the blood of Jesus has already absolved us.

It's not that our sin is unimportant. Jesus clearly wants us to confess our sins in prayer. But not before we have adored God as Father, worshipped Him as holy, prayed for His Kingdom to come, and even petitioned Him as Provider of our personal needs.

This is a glorious revelation for every believer. Our sin is not the first thing on God's mind when we come to Him in prayer. This frees us from the fear and condemnation that prevent many Christians from praying.

The writer of Hebrews affirms this:

> *"This High Priest of ours understands our weaknesses, for he faced all of the same testings we do, yet he did not sin. So let us come boldly to the throne of our gracious God. There we will receive his mercy, and we will find grace to help us when we need it most."*
>
> Hebrews 4:15–16 (NLT)

Once we've been reoriented to who Jesus is as our Mediator before God, and who God is as our Father, confession and repentance are no longer fearful. They become freeing, which is exactly the point of this part of the Lord's Prayer.

We are confessing not to a judge who's ready to punish us, but to a Father who knows our weakness. He is eager to forgive us, cleanse us, and heal us of sin's damaging effects.

Confession Flows from Sonship, Not Condemnation

Here's a key truth that reshapes how we approach God in prayer:

Our confidence in prayer does not come from our success in obeying God, but from our identity in Christ as children of God.

There is no need for any follower of Christ to live under a weight of condemnation. If you're praying slowly and reflectively through the Lord's Prayer, you're easily a half hour into prayer before you even reach the part where Jesus tells you to confess sin.

If we lack the revelation of who we are in Christ as children of God, we will carry a sin-consciousness that will make us hesitant to pray. We'll assume He's disappointed, disapproving, or distant, and we'll think we need to clean ourselves up before coming to Him.

This is why Jesus teaches us to start prayer not with "Forgive my sin, Lord," but with "*Our Father.*"

From Judge to Father

I had a conversation recently with a friend I met at the gym. He grew up Roman Catholic and we've caught up a few times to talk about faith. Over coffee, he confided in me that he struggles to connect with God.

So, I asked him, "When you think about God, what comes to mind first? Do you think of Him as a loving Father? An all-powerful Creator? Or a holy Judge?"

Without hesitation, he answered, "Definitely a Judge."

I gently pointed out that this might be at the core of his difficulty connecting with God. If we see God primarily as Judge, prayer will always feel like a courtroom – a place of fear and defence. But if we see God as Father, prayer becomes a conversation in the living room flowing out of close relationship.

RECONCILIATION WITH GOD AND PEOPLE

You speak very differently to a judge than to a father. You try to avoid a judge. You defend yourself before a judge. You fear punishment from a judge.

But your Father? You can go to Him with confidence. He loves you. He's for you. He doesn't want to punish you. He wants to restore you.

That's why the most important aspect of our identity in prayer is that we are children of God.

> *"So you have not received a spirit that makes you fearful slaves. Instead, you received God's Spirit when He adopted you as His own children. Now we call Him, 'Abba, Father.' For His Spirit joins with our spirit to affirm that we are God's children."*
>
> Romans 8:15–16 (NLT)

This means we never need to "clean ourselves up" before coming to God. We have already been adopted as sons and daughters. We stand before the Judge who, in Christ, has already declared us innocent. To keep showing up trying to re-defend ourselves is to miss the good news of the gospel.

I repeat... If you have trusted in Christ, the judgement has already been given. You have been declared innocent.

Imagine a person who had been legally declared innocent continuing to show up to court every week, trying to argue their case again. It would make no sense.

Jesus invites us to approach God with boldness, not because we are perfect, but because He was perfect, and because we are now His innocent and beloved children.

Yes, God will clean us up. Yes, He will discipline and sanctify us. But He does so as a Father, not as a judge. And that makes all the difference in how we approach Him.

Confessing Sins to Restore Relationship

From this revelation of our new identity as adopted children of God, Jesus invites us to regularly confess our sins. But sometimes we hesitate to bring our sins into the light because we fear that doing so will give God more reasons to reject us.

We must remember that just as a loving father would never reject his struggling child, God can never reject one He has already adopted.

We are never confessing our sins to be made right with God again. Sin does not cause us to lose our identity as children of God – that has already been secured.

We confess our sin to receive forgiveness, be cleansed of wrongdoing, and restore our feelings of closeness with God.

Back to the judge and father distinction… A judge's job is to determine guilt and pronounce punishment. A father's role is to nurture, restore, and call out potential.

Confession, then, is not about reestablishing our salvation – for that was never lost. It's about restoring intimacy. Our sin does not un-adopt us or un-justify us, but it can grieve the Holy Spirit and disrupt the joy of our fellowship with Him.

> *"And do not grieve the Holy Spirit of God, by whom you were sealed for the day of redemption. Let all bitterness and wrath and anger and clamour and slander be put away from you, along with all malice."*
> Ephesians 4:30–31 (ESV)

RECONCILIATION WITH GOD AND PEOPLE

We talk about "keeping short accounts" in marriage – dealing with small issues before they become big ones. Not because they make us unmarried, but because they affect intimacy. The same is true in our relationship with God.

> *"If we confess our sins, He is faithful and just to forgive us our sins and to cleanse us from all unrighteousness. If we say we have not sinned, we make Him a liar, and His word is not in us."*
>
> 1 John 1:9–10 (ESV)

Confession keeps our hearts soft. It cultivates humility and honesty. Ignoring sin hardens the heart and dulls our spiritual sensitivity. That's why God, like a loving Father, calls us to bring our sins into the light – not to shame us, but to heal us.

What Can Be Harder than Confessing Sin?

As hard as it can be to confess our own sin, it can be even more challenging to forgive the sins of others. Yet Jesus reveals that the two are intertwined. Giving forgiveness is essential because those who have truly received forgiveness will also become forgiving.

In verse 12 of the Lord's Prayer, Jesus frames our forgiveness of others as something already done – *"as we also have forgiven our debtors."* In other words, forgiving others is meant to be the normal posture of a forgiven child of God.

The posture from which we ask God for the forgiveness of our sins is the forgiveness we have already committed to extend to others.

When we choose to follow Christ, we relinquish all rights to bitterness. Holding grudges is not allowed in God's Kingdom.

As was highlighted at the start of this chapter – directly after the Lord's Prayer, Jesus circles back on the forgiveness issue. He says if we are unwilling to forgive others, it reveals that we have not truly or fully understood and received God's forgiveness ourselves.

If we truly see our own sin and the punishment we deserved, and then experience the grace that follows, it would be impossible to hold others in the debt of bitterness.

But when we lack revelation of God's forgiveness and Father-heart and instead live as if God is still our Judge, we are quick to become judges of others – critical, harsh, and unwilling to release.

Jesus makes this truth abundantly clear in the story of the Unforgiving Servant. A servant was forgiven a massive debt by his master but then refused to forgive a small debt owed to him by another. When the master learned of his servant's hypocrisy, he threw him in prison until he could pay back his full debt.

The point was clear: if we withhold forgiveness from others, we show we haven't truly grasped the mercy we've been given, and therefore we have missed God's forgiveness.

Forgiveness Must Be Forged

This kind of mercy doesn't happen by accident. It's forged in the fire of injustice, disappointment, and unmet expectations.

Jesus knows that forgiving those who hurt us will often be hard. That's why He commands it. Our flesh wants payback. But God says, "Let Me be your vindicator."

Importantly, Jesus doesn't say to forgive those who merely disappointed us. Sometimes what we call offence is really a case of unmet expectations, personality differences, or misunderstandings, but not actual sin.

That's why, when struggling to forgive, it's helpful to ask:

Was this truly a sin against me, or just a failure to meet my expectations?

Is this a personality difference that I find difficult and annoying, or has this person truly wronged me?

Being able to answer that question accurately is a sign of emotional and spiritual maturity. If we're just annoyed, or struggling with unmet expectations, there's probably nothing to forgive. We just need to change our perspective and choose to love the person.

But sometimes people truly do sin against us, and that can be emotionally painful, and it can feel very hard to forgive.

Real-Time Forgiveness

I was once preparing to preach on this very topic of forgiveness and found myself deeply tested in real time.

Funny story – I had been praying that week through the Lord's Prayer and thought to myself, "I don't really have anyone to forgive. I'm good." Then the test came.

Someone who was supposed to be a Christian brother – someone I had helped in many ways – sent me a message I'd be surprised to receive from my worst enemy. It was full of false accusations and abusive language, all cloaked in religious phrases with a prophetic tone.

My flesh wanted to fire back words that would crush him. But I suspected that he was projecting his own self-hatred upon me. So instead of being my own vindicator, I replied to say that I would take his accusations before the Lord, and that I would continue praying for God's blessing and prosperity over his future.

The next day, I made the decision to do just that. I brought his unkind message before the Lord. I asked the Holy Spirit to show me if any of his accusations were true. Some of the accusations brought up helpful prayer points for my own leadership growth. But most of what was written, the Holy Spirit told me to ignore.

Then I declared to God my forgiveness toward this man and asked Him to bless him and to be merciful in His loving discipline toward him.

This is how Jesus says we MUST deal with injustice and offence. We're not given any other option. Forgiving others is a simple choice. We either obey and forgive, or we disobey and grow bitter.

The next time someone wrongs you, try this little exercise: Bring their sin against you before the Lord. Ask Him how He sees it. Allow Him to refine you through it. Then choose to forgive the person considering how God has already forgiven you.

Do this, and you will feel the weight of unforgiveness and hurt lift off you.

Who Do You Need to Forgive?

Who was it that wronged you? Who do you need to forgive? Was it your father or mother? A sibling? A boss? A friend?

Did someone truly sin against you, or did you take up an offence that wasn't yours to carry?

If forgiveness feels hard to you, maybe the more urgent need is a deeper revelation of your own sin and the mercy, grace, and kindness that God has already extended to you.

Surely you wouldn't say that you deserve forgiveness while the person who sinned against you does not. That would sound a lot like the unforgiving servant in Jesus' story.

Are you keeping short accounts with the Holy Spirit? Are you willing to sit quietly before Him and allow Him to reveal what's in the dark?

Jesus became sin for us. He was punished on our behalf, so that we could be called children of God.

If you've never trusted in Christ and confessed your sins to God, there is no better time than now.

If there's someone you know you need to forgive, there is no better time than now.

Take a few minutes now to pray through the Lord's Prayer and spend some extra time on verse 12. Receive forgiveness from God and give forgiveness to anyone who comes to mind who has sinned against you.

Reflection Questions for Chapter 4

1. Do you see God more as a Judge or as a loving Father? How does this affect the way you approach confession?

2. Are there any unconfessed sins in your life that are affecting your intimacy with God? Are you willing to bring them into the light?

3. In what ways do you tend to hide or deflect responsibility for your sins? What would it look like to own them fully before God?

4. Is there someone in your life you need to forgive? What is holding you back?

5. Have you confused unmet expectations with being sinned

against? What distinction do you need to make in your heart?

6. When was the last time you brought an offence before the Lord and asked Him how He sees it?

7. What does it look like for you to keep "short accounts" with God and with others?

A Prayer for Receiving and Giving Forgiveness

Father, thank You that You have adopted me as Your child. I come to You today, not in shame, but with confidence that You love me. I confess my sins to You...

You already know all my sins, and yet You still receive me. Cleanse me, soften my heart, and restore my joy.

And Lord, I choose to forgive those who have hurt me...

Help me release bitterness, offence, and the desire to get even. I lay every wound and every word before You. Refine my heart and fill me with Your mercy. Teach me to walk in humility and honesty, that I can live in the freedom of Your love and grace.

Chapter Five

Overcoming the Darkness

Prayers for Freedom and Deliverance

Next in the Lord's Prayer, now that we've received and given forgiveness, Jesus says to pray,

> *"And lead us not into temptation, but deliver us from evil."*
>
> Matthew 6:13 (ESV)

The *New Living Translation* is helpful in clarifying Jesus' words:

> *"And don't let us yield to temptation but rescue us from the evil one."*
>
> Matthew 6:13 (NLT)

We Have a Deceptive Enemy

There's a line from a film released the same year I became a Christian, all the way back in 1995. It's called *The Usual Suspects* (note: there's a lot of violence and strong language, so parental guidance is suggested). One quote from the film struck a deep chord with me when I saw it as a young believer:

> *"The greatest trick the devil ever pulled was convincing the world that he doesn't exist."*
> Roger "Verbal" Kent (played by Kevin Spacey)

It's a haunting line, because it's true.

Scripture reveals that Satan often works behind the scenes, manipulating, deceiving, and operating in darkness. While billions of people around the world deny his existence, Paul says something shocking:

> *"Satan, who is the god of this world, has blinded the minds of those who don't believe."*
> 2 Corinthians 4:4 (NLT)

Those who reject Christ and deny Satan's existence are, in fact, under his influence. That's the brilliance (for him) and the danger (for us) of his deception.

As Christians, we would never outright say that we don't believe in the devil. But many Christians live as if he isn't real – ignorant of his schemes and indifferent to his attacks.

C.S. Lewis once said there are two equally dangerous but opposite errors we can make as Christians when it comes to the devil. The first is to give him too much credit, living in fear and paranoia. The second is to give him too little attention, ignoring or dismissing his influence entirely.

Jesus, in how He teaches us to pray here, gives us a balanced but powerful strategy to address the reality of the activity of our spiritual enemy.

Spiritual Warfare in the Lord's Prayer

Jesus tells us to pray,

> *"...Don't let us yield to temptation, but rescue us from the evil one."*
>
> Matthew 6:13 (NLT)

Notice, He doesn't say to yell at the devil (although sometimes I do like to yell at the devil) or perform deliverance rituals (although, as often as possible, I do seek to cast demons out of people).

Instead, He invites us to make the foundation of our spiritual warfare two essential and foundational points of prayer:

1. **Pray for protection from temptation** (the spiritual influence that entices the flesh).

2. **Pray for deliverance from the evil one** (rescue from Satan's schemes).

Who is Our Enemy?

A crucial first step in spiritual warfare is to know exactly who our enemy is. Paul helps us with this:

> *"We are not fighting against flesh-and-blood enemies, but against evil rulers and authorities of the unseen world…"*
>
> Ephesians 6:12 (NLT)

Even when a person seems like the enemy, we're told they're never the real problem. Behind most human sin and some relational conflict is an invisible spiritual enemy.

Furthermore, Satan is strategic. He studies us. He seeks to exploit our weaknesses. Paul warns us to be on guard so that:

> *"Satan might not outwit us. For we are not unaware of his schemes."*
>
> 2 Corinthians 2:11 (NIV)

We're told to stay alert, being aware of Satan's schemes. We're not to be fearful, but discerning.

Jesus knew this. And so, He teaches us to daily pray for two kinds of spiritual victory.

1. Pray for Protection from Temptation

This is a defensive prayer. Temptation is the devil's attempt to draw something out from within us – to bait the desires of the flesh. On our own, we are not strong enough to resist temptation to sin. That's why we must pray for God's help.

Remember, this call to pray for freedom from temptation comes immediately after we have confessed our sins and received forgiveness. Jesus invites us to ask for power that we might not go back to commit again the sins we just confessed. He wants us to walk in freedom and holiness moving forward.

Temptations will come, but we are not powerless. Paul says:

> *"God is faithful, and He will not let you be tempted beyond your ability, but with the temptation He will also provide the way of escape..."*
>
> 1 Corinthians 10:13 (ESV)

Asking for protection from temptation should become our daily acknowledgement of dependence on God for strength. We're saying, "Lord, don't let me fall again. Help me to see the way of escape You provide."

2. Pray for Deliverance from the Evil One

This is an offensive prayer. We're not just holding ground – we're taking it back.

Jesus invites us to ask the Father to rescue us from the grip, deception, and influence of Satan. This may involve personal strongholds – areas where we've yielded ground through sin, lies, unforgiveness, or fear. It may also involve praying for deliverance in our families, communities, or churches.

This prayer says, "God, take back what the enemy has stolen. Restore what has been lost. Push back darkness."

The first prayer protects the front door of the soul from future attacks. The second reclaims the back rooms the enemy may still be hiding in.

The Enemy Has Been Disarmed

Satan and his demons have already been ultimately defeated and fully disarmed by Jesus.

Spiritual warfare is not a cosmic battle between equal and opposite forces. This isn't *Star Wars*. There is no "balance" between light and dark.

God is uncreated, eternal, and all-powerful. Satan is a created being – limited, finite, and operating under permission.

Yes, Satan once exercised some authority in the nations due to humanity's rebellion. Adam surrendered his God-given authority, which left a void that the devil stepped into through his disobedience. That rebellion enabled Satan to rule illegitimately in God's world.

But God became a man in the person of Jesus Christ. Jesus lived without sin, died in our place, and rose again, conquering both sin and Satan. Paul declares this reality clearly:

> *"You were dead because of your sins and because your sinful nature was not yet cut away. Then God made you alive with Christ, for He forgave all our sins. He cancelled the record of the charges against us and took it away by nailing it to the cross. In this way, He disarmed the spiritual rulers and authorities. He shamed them publicly by His victory over them on the cross."*
> Colossians 2:13–15 (NLT)

Christ's victory on the cross was a victory over the demonic realm. From that moment, the kingdom of darkness has been publicly stripped of all authority.

The word Paul uses for "disarmed" is rich. In modern terms, it's like saying an enemy army has been completely stripped of both its armour and its ammunition.

Think about that for a moment: an enemy with no armour and no ammo has only one option remaining. Their only hope of victory is to bluff.

Our Bluffing Enemy

This brings to mind a scene from the classic WWII mini-series *Band of Brothers*. During the Battle of the Bulge at Bastogne, the 101st Airborne was dug in, surrounded, and nearly out of ammunition. Though the Germans continued firing mortar rounds at the Americans, they never fully advanced. Their hesitation bought just enough time for General Patton's Third Army to arrive and turn the tide.

By digging in and appearing strong, the 101st bluffed their way to victory at a critical turning point in WWII.

Many of us are a little like the Germans in prayer. We might lob a few "mortar rounds" of prayer at the enemy, occasionally inflicting some damage, but because we lack daily prayer against the enemy, we fail to advance. Meanwhile, the enemy bluffs, hoping we don't realise how weak and defeated he truly is.

When the enemy holds ground in our lives, families, churches, or cities, it's not because he is strong. It's because we aren't yet advancing in prayer.

Jesus taught us to pray "deliver us from the evil one" precisely because this is how ground is taken back. Prayer is the starting point of Kingdom advance. If we don't pray, he holds his bluff. If we do, he flees. James speaks of this:

> *"Submit yourselves therefore to God. Resist the devil, and he will flee from you."*
>
> James 4:7 (ESV)

The word "resist" here is more aggressive than it sounds in English. The Greek means to stand against, to oppose actively, to set oneself in direct opposition. This isn't passive resistance. It's active warfare.

The Prayerlessness of the Church

The only power Satan can retain is the prayerlessness of God's people.

When we live as if the devil doesn't exist – or when we fail to engage him in prayer – we allow him to hold ground. But when we pray as Jesus taught, we actively resist and push him back.

Could it be that much of the darkness in our cities, our culture, and even the Church exists because we haven't stood in prayerful resistance?

Most of us say we believe that spiritual warfare is important, but the evidence of that belief is found in our habitual daily prayer against the enemy.

Jesus has already won. The enemy has already been defeated. Our job now is to enforce this victory on the cross through our daily prayer.

Common Footholds the Enemy Exploits

OVERCOMING THE DARKNESS

Here are seven common footholds the enemy often tries to exploit in God's people. These are points of vulnerability – open doors where his influence can creep in if left unguarded. Recognising and closing these footholds through repentance, forgiveness, and prayer is a vital step in walking in the freedom Christ has already won for us.

1. Unrepentant Sin

Habitual sin – especially sexual immorality, addiction, or other areas of overt compromise – will give the enemy ground. We can't expect spiritual victory if we are unwilling to let go of sinful habits.

Sin will keep the door open to the enemy. Close any doors that are open through confession and repentance. In most cases, habitual sin needs to be confessed to a trusted pastor or someone who can help you find healing.

> *"Submit to God, resist the devil, and he will flee."*
> James 4:7 (ESV)

2. Past Trauma or Abuse

Trauma isn't sin, but it creates wounds where lies can take root. If we have been sinned against, we might struggle with self-talk like, "I'm worthless," or "I'll never be safe."

Bringing these wounds of abuse into the light by sharing with a trusted Christian friend or counsellor can be very freeing.

Jesus came...

> *"... to set the oppressed free."*
>
> Luke 4:18 (NIV)

3. Unforgiveness

This should have already been dealt with in the previous part of the Lord's Prayer. But if you hold on to offence and refuse to forgive, that unforgiveness will become a foothold for demonic activity.

Remember, forgiveness in the Kingdom of God is not optional. Unforgiveness is the devil's playground.

In Ephesians 4, Paul links unresolved anger and bitterness to demonic influence:

> *"Be angry and do not sin; do not let the sun go down on your anger, and give no opportunity to the devil."*
>
> Ephesians 4:26–27 (ESV)

4. Generational Strongholds

Sin patterns are often passed down through family lines. Sometimes generational curses need to be broken through prayer.

If you suspect you are struggling with habitual sin or other consequences because of a generational stronghold, seek a trusted Christian who can lead your through prayers of deliverance.

Scripture often speaks of the generational consequences to sin, but thankfully, God also offers us generational mercy.

Referring to the worship of idols, He says:

> *"You shall not bow down to them or serve them, for I the Lord your God am a jealous God, visiting the iniquity of the fathers on the children to the third and the fourth generation of those who hate me, but showing steadfast love to thousands of those who love me and keep my commandments."*
>
> Exodus 20:5–6 (ESV)

5. Occult Practices and False Religions

Practices like witchcraft, astrology, Freemasonry, occult healing, or tarot cards are not spiritually neutral. Dabbling in these will open doors to the enemy.

These strongholds will need to be broken through prayer.

We see a great example in Acts 19 of the gospel confronting the culture of witchcraft in first century Ephesus. Early believers burned their books of magic publicly.

> *"A number of them who had been practicing sorcery brought their incantation books and burned them at a public bonfire. The value of the books was several million dollars. So the message about the Lord spread widely and had a powerful effect."*
>
> Acts 19:19–20 (NLT)

6. False Inner Vows

Phrases like "I'll never trust anyone again" create walls that harden the heart and resist God's help. Our words have power, and in nearly all cases, deeply rooted declarations must be broken through prayer.

> *"For the weapons of our warfare are not of the flesh but have divine power to destroy strongholds. We destroy arguments and every lofty opinion raised against the knowledge of God, and take every thought captive to obey Christ,"*
>
> 2 Corinthians 10:4–5 (ESV)

7. Soul Ties or Unholy Bonds

Emotional or sexual connections formed outside of God's design can entangle us spiritually. Sexual intimacy and unholy covenants form bonds that may need to be broken through renunciation and deliverance prayer.

Paul warns that sexual sin is not just a physical act but a spiritual union. He quotes Genesis 2:24 (*"the two shall become one flesh"*) to show that sexual intimacy creates a bond that should only exist within marriage.

> *"Or do you not know that he who is joined to a prostitute becomes one body with her? For, as it is written, 'The two will become one flesh.'"*
>
> 1 Corinthians 6:16 (ESV)

This principle holds true with any sexual encounter outside of marriage, not just with a prostitute.

If you need freedom in this area, and many of us have, find someone that you trust, someone who is not living in sexual sin, to pray for you and help you access freedom and a new start in Christ.

Freedom Is Our Inheritance in Christ

Christ came to set us free from all the works of the enemy. Paul declares this to the Colossian church.

> *"He has delivered us from the domain of darkness and transferred us to the kingdom of His beloved Son, in whom we have redemption, the forgiveness of sins."*
> Colossians 1:13–14 (ESV)

Jesus has already delivered us. But He also calls us to appropriate that deliverance daily through prayer.

Deliverance begins first in our own lives, then radiates outward – into our families and the world around us. As we find freedom ourselves, God can use us to help set others free from the grip of the enemy.

Helpful Questions to Discern Entry Points of Evil:

Ask yourself the following questions to consider whether the enemy may have a stronghold in your life that needs deliverance.

- Is there a recurring pattern of sin, fear, or relational dysfunction?

- Are there parts of your past that still feel "charged" with shame or pain?

- Have you ever made vows or believed lies that contradict the gospel?

- Have you or your family participated in occult or false religious practices?

- Are there generational sins that you can see in your family line?

- Is there someone you still deeply resent or have not forgiven?

If necessary, bring all these things into the light. If someone is discipling you, ask them to pray over these things with you. To get free, we often benefit from the help of someone else who is already free. We can leverage their authority in prayer so we can walk in new liberty ourselves.

And remember – Jesus has already won the victory!

Reflection Questions for Chapter 5

1. Are you regularly asking God to help you resist temptation? In what areas do you most need His grace today?

2. Have you unknowingly given the enemy a foothold in any area of your life? What might those areas be?

3. Do you tend to view spiritual warfare more passively (defensive) or actively (offensive)? Why?

4. Have you experienced repeated struggles or patterns that

could be rooted in past wounds or generational strongholds?

5. Is there anything in your life (bitterness, lies, vows, soul ties) that you need to renounce and bring under the authority of Christ?

A Prayer for Freedom from the Enemy

Father, thank You that Jesus has already defeated the enemy. Thank You that I am no longer a slave to sin or under the devil's authority. Today, I ask for Your power to resist temptation. Strengthen me where I am weak and expose any foothold the enemy may have gained in my life.

Deliver me from the enemy's power and help me to see every evil scheme he may attempt to bring against me. Lead me into deeper freedom and greater power and authority over darkness. Use me, Lord, to bring deliverance and freedom into the lives of others.

Chapter Six
Finishing Strong
Prayers of Praise

We've now come to the final line of the Lord's Prayer, where we read an addition from the early church that provokes us to end our time of prayer as we began – by exalting God.

> *"For Yours is the Kingdom, and the power, and the glory, forever. Amen."*
>
> Matthew 6:13 (ESV)

Although not found in the earliest manuscripts of Matthew's Gospel, this final doxology was added by the early church and became part of Christian liturgy as early as the second century – and for good reason.

This closing line is a fitting and Spirit-inspired response to the whole prayer. As the Lord's Prayer teaches us how to approach God with worship and make our requests to Him in the right order, this doxology shows us how to finish strong in prayer: not with fear, worry, or even a petition, but with worshipful praise.

Where This Line Came From

This final doxology is deeply rooted in Scripture. It echoes King David's closing prayer when he transferred leadership of the nation of Israel to his son Solomon:

> *"Yours, O Lord, is the greatness and the power and the glory and the victory and the majesty, for all that is in the heavens and in the earth is yours. Yours is the kingdom, O Lord, and you are exalted as head above all."*
>
> 1 Chronicles 29:11 (ESV)

By ending the Lord's Prayer with this line of praise, the early church was doing what all believers should learn to do – end every time of prayer with humble surrender and with recognition of God's greatness as our focus.

Our praise keeps God supreme in our hearts.

We Praise for Perspective

Praise has a way of reshaping how we see the world.

It reorients our thoughts toward truth. It drowns out the lies of the enemy. It strengthens our faith as we declare who God is and what He's like. It keeps God in His rightful place – on the throne of our hearts.

King David, in a moment of praise himself says,

> *"...you are holy, enthroned on the praises of Israel."*
> Psalm 22:3 (ESV)

David uncovered a profound truth here. When we praise, we give God the ruling seat over our lives, our homes, our workplaces, our church, and our circumstances.

That's why many of the Psalms begin with lament or need but end with praise.

Psalm 13 begins with:

> *"How long, O Lord? Will You forget me forever?"*
> Psalm 13:1 (ESV)

But it ends with:

> *"I will sing to the Lord, because He has dealt bountifully with me."*
> Psalm 13:6 (ESV)

This is the shape of many heartfelt prayers. They begin in desperation and dependence, but finish with declarations of truth and praise.

In this last line of the Lord's Prayer, there's a reason why these three points of praise are given – kingdom, power, and glory. Each highlights an important aspect of the worship we should offer God in the light of who He is.

"Yours is the Kingdom"
A Declaration of Submission and Allegiance

When we say, "Yours is the Kingdom," we are proclaiming that God reigns. He is the highest authority. He rules over our own ideas, over rebellious political powers, over ungodly cultural influences, and especially over the enemy who has already been defeated.

Declaring that God's Kingdom belongs to Him is an act of surrender: "I lay down my right to rule, my agenda, and my reputation. Jesus, You alone rule."

This praise sounds like:

- "Jesus, You are Lord over my life and my future."

- "Your rule is perfect; I trust Your leadership."

- "I lay down my will so that Your Kingdom comes in me and through me."

Our praise dethrones self and enthrones Christ.

"Yours is the Power"
A Declaration of Trust and Dependence

When we say, "Yours is the power," we are declaring that God is infinitely able. He has the power to provide, to forgive, to deliver, and to save. This line lifts our eyes from our own weakness to His strength.

This praise sounds like:

- "Nothing is too hard for You, Lord."

- "Your strength is made perfect in my weakness."

- "You uphold the universe by the word of Your power."

Declaring that our power comes from Him confronts the idol of self-reliance and reminds us that what we need in response to our prayers is His grace – not more hard work and effort from ourselves.

Paul saw this when he said:

> *"Now to Him who is able to do far more abundantly than all that we ask or think, according to the power at work within us,"*
>
> Ephesians 3:20 (ESV)

Knowing that God is infinitely able empowers us to rest and be at peace in Him as we wait for answered prayer.

"Yours is the Glory"
A Declaration of Who is Worthy

Finally, we say, "Yours is the glory." This is about who gets the fame, the honour, and the credit.

This line brings the entire prayer full circle. We began with "*hallowed be Your name*" – a declaration of worship in the light of God's holiness. Now we end in a similar way by saying, "All glory belongs to You."

This kind of praise sounds like:

- "All I have, all I've done, all I hope for – it's all Yours."

- "Not to us, O Lord, not to us, but to Your name be the glory."

- "May Jesus be made famous through my life."

Paul shows us how natural it is to offer this kind of praise. At the end of Romans 11, he was so overcome by the truth he was writing that he said,

> *"For from Him and through Him and to Him are all things. To Him be glory forever."*
> Romans 11:36 (ESV)

Praise changes us. It reminds us of who we are praying to. It re-aligns our perspective. And it ensures our time alone with God never becomes just a self-centred wish list.

Reflection Questions for Chapter 6

1. Do you tend to finish prayer once you've made your final request?

2. In what areas of your life do you need to declare, "Yours is the Kingdom"?

3. Where are you tempted to rely on your own strength instead of God's power?

4. Have you been taking credit for something when the glory really belongs to God?

5. How might your life look different if you regularly made these three declarations of praise every time your prayed?

A Prayer of Praise

Father, thank You for hearing every word I've brought before You today in prayer.

Yours is the Kingdom. You reign over my life, over every circumstance, and over every nation of the world. I submit my will to Yours and trust Your perfect leadership.

Yours is the power. You alone can provide, save, heal, and deliver. I confess that I am weak, but You are strong. I put my confidence in You today.

Yours is the glory. Let Your name be lifted high in my life. Let my words, my work, and my worship bring You honour. I don't seek the spotlight – my greatest desire is that the name of Jesus would be made known.

Amen

Chapter Seven
Developing a Discipline of Daily Prayer
Putting It All Into Practice

You've reached the end of this book, but hopefully the beginning of a new discipline of daily prayer in your life. Before you embark on this journey, it's important to consider a few important practical points as you develop your own daily practice of prayer.

In Luke's gospel, we find the companion passage to the Lord's Prayer in Matthew. One part in particular stands out

> *"When you pray, say..."*
>
> Luke 11:2 (ESV)

He didn't say *if* you pray, but *when* you pray. When Jesus spoke about prayer, he assumed prayer would be a regular part of our lives.

And that shouldn't be a surprise. How else could we truly grow in relationship with God?

Therefore, the prayer that Jesus taught us was not meant to be merely studied. It is more than bullet points of truth.

The Lord's Prayer was given to help us form a rhythm of regular daily prayer, and to approach Him with the right priorities. Through it, the Holy Spirit helps us to grow beyond just sporadic bursts of self-centred prayer.

In the introduction, we reflected on how the disciples didn't ask Jesus to teach them to preach, to lead, or to heal. They said, *"Lord, teach us to pray."* They saw Jesus draw away many times to be alone with God, and they knew that this discipline of prayer was the source of His peace and His power.

So how do we build this kind of consistent prayer life?

The answer is pretty simple, but not necessarily easy. Just set a daily appointment with God and keep it. All we have to do is show up consistently.

It's not going to be perfect at first. In fact, it will probably never be perfect. But it must become consistent.

The first thing to do is to make a start, and if you miss a day, or even a week, just get started again.

As we said at the beginning of this book, none of us will ever get to the point where we feel like we've mastered prayer. We'll always be seeking to grow closer to God. It's a lifetime practice of continual improvement, greater levels of focus, and deeper communion with Christ.

What's most important is making the initial decision to spend time with God every single day.

Daily Rhythms of Prayer

Back to Martin Luther... He said,

> "It is a good thing to let prayer be the first business of the morning and the last at night."
>
> Martin Luther

You don't need to become a monk or set aside three hours of prayer each day. You just need to commit to developing rhythms every day, and ideally throughout your day.

The Lord's Prayer can fit easily into the schedules of real life. It can be prayed in two minutes, over twenty minutes, or even over two hours.

Here are a few ways to build rhythms of prayer with the Lord into your daily routine:

1. In the Morning - Start Your Day with God

As soon as you wake up (or better yet, after you've poured your morning coffee), but before the noise of daily life begins, set aside time to meditate on God's Word.

Then slowly pray through the Lord's Prayer. Sit with each line. Think about what you've learned in this book. Pray whatever words come to your mind as the Holy Spirit guides you.

2. At Lunch - A Midday Reset

Pause during your lunch break. Go for a short walk, or just close your office door.

Even just 3 to 5 minutes praying through the Lord's Prayer will re-centre your soul. Say the Prayer aloud, let each line spark a fresh prayer. Or just let the Holy Spirit highlight one line to focus on for the entire time.

If you haven't figured it out yet, it's very important to memorise the Lord's Prayer. That way, you always have it on the tip of your tongue, ready to pray from the heart.

3. At Night - Rest in the Lord Before You Sleep

As your head hits the pillow, end the day with the Lord's Prayer on your lips. Often, I never make it past adoring and worshipping the Father before I drift off to sleep.

If you happen to make it all the way through the Prayer, go back and pick something to pray about more deeply. It might be a lost friend or family member, a personal need, or something at work that feels stressful.

What better way to fall asleep than in communion with God?

A Final Word of Warning

As helpful and powerful as the Lord's Prayer is, it's important that we not become too rigid.

I was speaking to someone recently who said that she sometimes finds herself praying through the Lord's Prayer, then thinks about something else she wants to pray about, but says to herself, "Oh wait, I can't talk to God about that yet because I need to first pray through each point of the Lord's Prayer."

While the order of the Lord's Prayer is purposeful, it's right and good to let the Holy Spirit guide you. You should always feel free to go off script.

Go ahead and allow yourself to be caught up in Spirit-led times of free prayer. You can always come back to the Lord's Prayer if you're not sure what to pray for next.

Our highest goal in prayer should be Spirit-led prayer.

And don't forget to keep times of prayer very relational. Don't be afraid to talk to God honestly, spontaneously, and freely. The Lord's Prayer is more of a compass than a track you are restricted to.

There will be times when you pray every line slowly and intentionally. And there will be other times when you have run out of time to pray and you're only partially through the Lord's Prayer. Either way, it's all good!

Jesus didn't give us this prayer to restrict us. He gave it to empower us to connect deeply with God. Anytime that happens, you are winning in prayer, even if you're not praying the Lord's Prayer.

Reflection Questions for Chapter 7

1. What time of day are you most alert and least distracted? Can you commit that time to daily prayer?

2. Which line of the Lord's Prayer speaks most powerfully to your current season of life?

3. Where in your day - morning, midday, or evening - can you begin praying the Lord's Prayer regularly?

4. What barriers have kept you from consistent prayer in the past? How can this structure help overcome them?

5. Who in your life could you encourage or teach to pray using the Lord's Prayer?

A Prayer for Consistency and Freedom in Prayer

Father, make me a person of consistent prayer. Help me to not just say the words, but Holy Spirit empower me to pray from a deep place.

Help me to be faithful to start each day in prayer, and to connect with you consistently throughout the day.

Help me to focus upon you in the last moments of my day. May I drift off to sleep every night with words to you on my lips.

Lord Jesus, teach me to pray.

About the author

Jason Staggers and his wife Olivia are the senior leaders of Ascend Church in Perth, Western Australia. To learn more about Ascend Church, visit *ascend.org.au*.

www.ingramcontent.com/pod-product-compliance
Lightning Source LLC
Chambersburg PA
CBHW042128100526
44587CB00026B/4217